THE RETURNING WAVE

THE

RETURNING

WAVE

Sonnets & other poems

Lucy Beckett

Ampleforth Abbey Press
(Distributed by Gracewing)

AMPLEFORTH ABBEY PRESS
AMPLEFORTH ABBEY
YORK
from
Gracewing
Fowler Wright Books
Southern Avenue, Leominster
Herefordshire HR6 0QF

ISBN 0 85244 364 1

Typeset at Ampleforth Abbey in Monotype Bembo
Printed at the Cromwell Press, Broughton Gifford,
Melksham, Wiltshire, SN12 8PH.

Contents

The great church: the crypt at Ripon
for C.C.E.

Under the great church
in the ancient dark
of badgers · Saxons · and the broken spears
of thrashed defenders at the river crossing
in stone space
thickwalled against the moving earth
a boat of silence
thirteen hundred years
hidden
empty now · the tomb
of the body of God.

Later an old man saying Mass
so old he falters · almost falls
frail at the altar as a winter leaf
sure in his hands
the body of God.

Incarnation

Be hidden as the limestone hides the spring,
as winter hides the flower, the bee, the plum
in silence, and behind the funeral bark
hides all the leaves that summer will become.
Be covert as the lily in the dark
hold of the earth till her unfastening
and as the river under ice, be dumb.

The dead of winter is the time of death,
of absence, exile, of no life, we say.
Autumn was that, autumn was when the corn
turned white and buckled, when a soft decay
rotted the grapes, the roses from the thorn,
when one by one the leaves without a breath
of wind to twitch them homeward dropped to clay.

Autumn was when they died. The winter frost
chars them to shifting ash from which will seep
upwards the sap to string the summer's shade
over the cattle and their fly-hung sleep.
O love forget the feasting August made.
Harvests are buried in stone fields, and lost
among flints the vines their crimson keep.

As arctic hares travel the empty snow
white as the snow to hide their flesh, their fear,
from hawk and fox, be silent when you touch
first with your speaking fingers this your dear
made world, be mute within our mortal hutch
a while; for we, though we shall never know
more than you tell us, soon will pounce, will tear

your flesh and spend your blood. Your death will hide,
even as your birth, one among many ears
of buckled corn, one among many leaves
fallen to winter dust. Love disappears,
goes out, hanging, a rebel between thieves.
Then bread was ash again: all of us died,
spilt with the wine into the turning years.

No, but it was not so. Because you came
into the quick and dying of the world,
and, quick and dying as the grapes, the corn,
spoke in their flesh, our flesh, and live, a curled
and crumpled glory hides still to be born
in every seed of winter, and the same
banner of Easter in the womb lies furled.

Requiem

Deh, fammiti vedere in ogni loco:
Se da mortal bellezza arder mi sento,
appresso al tuo mi sara foco ispento,
e io nel tuo caro, com'ero, in foco.   (Michelangelo)

I

In the spring I shall find
in the ruined cloister
in the early morning
the past which is next
as then and now
to eternity.

Old oak hard as iron
will be days in the burning;
rafter by rafter they heave the roof in,
crash together the echoes of psalms,
icy mornings, autumnal vespers
roar in the pit as the sparks scatter,
burn to an empty sky.

4

Everything that would sell was sold
and afterwards everything that would burn
was burnt, leaving stone, leaving
bone, to stand the weather
and the imperceptible crush of the hill.
Only flesh sees and touches
mortal beauty, as the breasts of pigeons.

Timbers, panelling, rushes, rope,
the psalters of every day, the pages
hands had turned, and the hands,
eyes, mouths, hearts, burned
in the crackling pit with the roofbeams
the monks watched burn before
the scattering of bones.

Over the choir arches in the April sun
the weak light catching turning wings,
the pigeons wheel and scatter and return
like charred fragments after the fire is cold,
burnt like parchment, lighter than parchment,
tatters, ashes, black cindery pigeons
gold in the light like souls.
  The history of God
   is hung on the bones of men.
    ad te omnis caro veniet

II

Old eyes watching what they cannot see
read to the bone.

Titian at ninety paints with his fingers
the teeth of hounds at his wrists, side, throat
the paint like lumps of blood and the flayers' knives
already at his skin.
In their time no fingers drew more life
from its exquisite surfaces. Now
they have none left for the fall of velvet,
blue quilted silk, breast-plate glint.

Actaeon who had surprised the goddess naked
drops as the hounds reach him, his head
already a beast's, his foothold lost
on the wet rocks. Marsyas
the satyr, the fool, one day took his flute
and had the temerity to outplay Apollo.
Knives strip his shaggy skin off from his flesh.
A dog licks up his blood. An old man fixes
his eyes on the dead face hung upside down.

The gods are jealous of such eyes, such fingers,
mortal invaders of their sovereignty.
Who risks a love thus undefended
shall to the pack be thrown, strung to the knife,
beaten with staves and have his flesh with thorns,
nails, spearpoint, pierced and torn.

This flesh is touch, taste, hearing, sight,
the flat of the hand on the warm earth,
and shall be to the fire that bore it borne.

At nightfall Titian the gentiluomo
watches the duck fly low
over the lagoon into the rising mist.
The beating of their wings besets his senses.
There is plague in the district of Santa Croce.
He only believed in death.

Three canvasses stand against the wall:
the third is a Pieta.
An old man keeps his eyes on the dead face.
The brushes are put away, but in the dusk
he dips his fingers into crimson paint.

III

The man born blind
sees because
the earth is mixed
with the spittle of God.
'Go away', they said,
'You liar.'

To the old leaving
all flesh is dying
given and ruined
made and killed
for a glimpse by a glimpse
of God.

IV

The field is the world
said the truth;
let us dig in it.

Touch with your fingers moss on the fallen stone
turf over living rock, stone, bone of the earth
and the fire far under.
Touch with your fingers
through the flesh of her fingers finger
by finger joint by joint the bone
the earth, through the flesh of her back
the ribs that will crumble.
Draw with your fingers over her cheekbones
her thin flesh while her eyes
are open. Where will the eyes go
where the souls that the eyes tell of
hers and yours when your fingers
and hers are bone?
All flesh is grass.

V

Old eyes read to the bone.

These eyes, these fingers for fifty years
drew from the life. Now
they have no time for the hero leapt from the tomb,
for the still no less
moving perfection of muscles under the skin.
Six days before his death Michelangelo
attacks with fury the body that carries sin,
chips at the dead limbs broken out of stone.
He hammers all night, a candle strapped to his head,
the body God broke, and breaks, he has broken,
the death that will never be finished
and Mary his mother with the grief she bears.
(The old were holding the young in their arms,
the living the dead.
That was how it was.)

Sparks fly from the chisel blade into the gathering dark
fire from the cold stone, mortal beauty
with the nails pulled from it, spent
the destructive flame.

At dawn the blows stop. In gaining light
he sips from a cup of water, lets drop
the chisel. He sees the body of Christ
dead, bearing the living on his back,
become the living who bears all the dead
his mother and all of us.
Michelangelo with his eyes on the dead face
sees the fire that bore him mortal beauty
that will burn and burnt
and burns his fire. He sees
the hand of God under his hand,
the dead limbs broken out of stone
on the third day.

VI

Over the cloister
the pigeons scatter
sparks of fire.

These old eyes
are centuries
blind in the grave

here and elsewhere
Venice and Rome:
look with them.

Veni sancte Spiritus
et emitte caelitus
lucis tuae radium

next to your fire
ours shall be spent
and we in your fire,

the living, the dying,
the hand and eye
of mortal beauty
as we have been shall be.

Requiem aeternam
dona eis Domine
et lux perpetua
luceat eis.

MEDITATION ON THE SEVEN SACRAMENTS

I

Baptism

His life, air, water, fire, he gives his earth
to print as his this, every, child God's thumb
spins to his image in his mother's womb;
a cupful of the river of Christ's death
that will lap over him rinses his head,
and air to spirit, fire to candle flame
are spoken, lit, by us who bring him home
son, brother of the firstborn from the dead.
Fingers too frail to bruise a butterfly
that will husk wheat, flinch at the barley's chafe
stroked backwards, tighten at the misery
of the world's grief inflicted in the lost
of God; our father, stamp your patience safe
on all their foreheads that your thorns have blessed.

II

Confirmation

Out of the desert, out of the red sand
which feeds no corn blade in the dancing heat
of devils' laughter, grips with sap no root
of holiness firm in the shifting ground
but parches throats, mocks eyes with dazzle, dulls
ears with the thud of violent dreams, lead us,
O Lord, touch us to hear where your springs rise
high in the dark cracks of your bracken hills
bubbling without sound out of ancient rock.
He brought them down the mountain: Tell no one
what you have seen, he said; Peter had known
him before glory poured out of the sky.
Mark your truth in us that when we turn back
no braver than he was, we also cry.

III

Marriage

Unless he turn our water into wine,
our flesh to his, poor pilgrims on the earth
and of it, brittle clay pots with our death
fired hard into us, and also divine
unreachable except in him our free
fragility, the storms we look to brave
in our foolhardiness ourselves to prove
our selves will smash us and the breaking sea
rattle to edgeless pebbles the sharp bits
of who we thought we were; till we have known
him walk the waves to us and the storm turn
under the tact of God to join our hearts
in given forgiven love, we shall not learn
it was his garden we took for our own.

Holy Orders

My son, into your hands, your flesh and blood
I made to harvest, grind, knead, bake my corn
and prune my vineyards, I commend my own
body and blood, into your mouth my word
to heal in men the evil that they do
before the blazing swords of angels burn
from them the weeds my enemy has sown
to feed their hunger for me. I give you
the mending of their brokenness · and hear
your own, another man, their other Christ,
flawed as you are · yet · you shall set them free,
oil on your hands the nailmarks of my priest;
beneath this cup my hand cradles your fear
that Pharoah's chariots hurled into the sea.

V

Eucharist

Crush in your fingers small seedheads the heat
of August bleaches of their sap; the world
faint in the thin high blare of drought grows old
unnourished as hot dust. What will you eat
starved children of my father to whose word
given to feed you you deafen your ears?
With seedcorn in your hands you go in tears
hearing complexities you have preferred
to me. Where are your simple senses? Sow
your corn and bring your harvest home with song.
Day after day die with me as the seed
is sacrificed in the dark earth below
your blinded sight, the life for which you long
is yours in my blood · my body · your bread.

VI

Penance

Wherever you have been · I have been there
there with the innocent you hurt, the weak
you were too strong and careless for, the sick
you did not stay awake with, fools, the poor
you made poorer, the victims of your power
to torture, leave alone, laugh at, to kill.
'Listen to him'; but you set out for hell
shouting the going was easy. I was there
with you also. I harrowed hell for you
calling my goats to come out of the din
the unmaking and unmarking fires they chose
themselves · to derelict my promise in.
And now you are here, and go, still free to lose
me. Not in the wastes of time will I lose you.

VII

The anointing of the sick

What have you done with truth? What have your eyes,
ears, hands, mouth, that have learnt, heard, tasted, seen
of God, here in his world, here in his son,
made, what have you made of his life, his days
he gave you to look, wait, for him in, speak
of him, carry his word in you, let, let
his will be done? Not with his sword to cut
justly your stone heart from you, not to break
your pride, your stubborn will under his wheel
of suffering does he at this frontier come
this edge of exile · but with oil to heal
your senses, mend his own, his mark, in you
his cross his mercy · which way you must go
only he knows · but either brings you home.

Cathedral in October

To sketch that afternoon
as with a wet brush on rough-grained paper
as with a flute

smoke on the mild air
grey watery lines · an English afternoon
no traffic near the cathedral
allowed
nevertheless at the blind narrow-arched high towers
pigeons home from the sky

barren Virginia creeper leaves against brick walls
thin vines · are crimson muted
they fall
singly and without sound to blackened lawns
not with the thud of apples
but of their own lack

soothed only · not tamed
the fox the Spartan boy kept hidden in his shirt
the self with its quick teeth
insists
even refining the inflections of its craving
to an extreme fineness

greedily it insists
here its familiar voices
utter the apple's roundness · arrow flight of pigeons
utter the lucid justice of their having
voices of Satan
insist

the lines are mixing one into another
hesitant · the music
to suffer a kind of death · a loosening of the grasp
a greeting given death
a fall
soundless as leaf-fall

of the assembled self that seemed as if it had
the ripeness of an apple
the satisfied direction
of a flown bird to its high throaty roost
bright blades
a clear intelligence

darken in autumn · soften · falter · undefine
all shape and end and sharpness
smoke from the heaps of leaves
seeps upward without flame
or spark
for what is burning burns invisibly

lose that you may be found
quiet in the melting night
the brush still · the flute
the smoke rising like prayer out of the burning year
and on your heart the fox · but not for long · asleep.

Sonnet in Advent

The angels' knowledge of the primordial being of things is called morning knowledge; and this is according as things exist in the Word. But their knowledge of the very thing created, as it stands in its own nature is called evening knowledge. St Thomas Aquinas

As never in summer · grief at the dying day
bits of his glory only he can mend
sharp in my hands · time given · time taken away
half understood · let fall · his hidden end
beyond the turning earth · the sun gone down
like honey on trees beside the lake · poems mist
breathed on glass · prisoners half freed from stone
a prelude listened to with tears and lost.

As never in summer · sorrow in the love
half lived · that catches at its quick the flame
of God · the morning world · the never enough
of longing for all beauty whole in him
who in the winter of the heart will come
and take our fractured love into his love.

Northumbrian time

A path back between cornfields and the sea:
hooked spines of barley grate against my thumb,
you spit through your teeth husks of bitten wheat,
black rocks beside us slabbed and seamed by water
dull to cracked paving as the tide goes out;
children took ears of corn and ate like this
and conscript soldiers and the monks who lie
in their salt graves where larks sing after rain
and the nap of the grass lies flat as silk.

Castle and headland fall to the cold waves
grey and white as the screaming gulls turning
planing from raucous ledges on the wind
under our feet where the flowery purple
uncut hay stops at the cliff edge; far down
black cormorants fly level with the tide,
the carrion tide falling to ebb that washed
the bodies of dead soldiers from the rocks
mixing their small warm blood into the sea.

Inland the snows and springs of the North Tyne
rang with centurions, Vikings, Scots raiding,
burning, building; under the dangerous ground
an emperor's remote cruel pride inscribed
on stone and wrenched from his quelled frontier roofs
six feet of secret darkness: floating wicks
flickered on bread, wine, words read, careful hands,
a mine of light shrouded in time, buried
in him and in him broken from the earth.

Altars stand empty, empty as the cross,
in foundered aisles and chancels, in the holes
narrow as sepulchres where Mass was said
within the thickness of a wall; the rain
blows through the bones of them like sand, like time
silting them deep in absence. Their bloom yet
is of a presence, present, gift beyond
the wrecks time rots, Christ's love the death of death
and tears that cloud it our imperfectness.

The returning wave

Learn how poor your flesh is, how not in courage
or any such fling of feeling it nets death
but lets death go · by · keeping still in knowledge
only that God is hungry for the breath
of truth he breathed in you, what has been good
and will be, all his gifts, his clarity
in your perceiving him in bread, in blood,
and trawls you deep for his own quality,
for where we stay each other, for his love;
so heaven floods the heartbeat days he came
to change, the muddled rocks where you must live
your life out in the hope that will become
shining and certain, the returning wave,
your flesh Christ's tent on the seashore of time.

Solway tide

Quietly the mud ticks after the sea retreats
drying while the silver edge goes, rustles beyond
sound, two miles back, back, and mud gives to the touch
a dinted mate wasting till the sea returns.

Skin-deep is deepest, of a kind to sense
itself skin-deep, and soft under foot, shore wind
out of September fields, blackberries bitten,
corn cut, later a hand laid on a stone wall:

touch the warm surface, skin of the steady earth
alive though the stubble fields are empty, left,
all rabbits shot that scattered, bare as the mud,
over the crying gulls float separate and high.

Long long till the tide comes back and the plough turns
pulling under the furrow the scrannel stalks
and the sea under its shining the dulled mud
covering the parched cockles and the hollow straw,

and gathered out of the sky the hungry gulls
will spill in the plough's wake and along the sea
come close now, very close so that the spring wheat
will lick at your ankles like the travelled tide.

Landscape with figure: Tuscany

Come down into the sun the round hills cry,
the silver hills, the olive groves, the foxes,
look how the ripe seed drops into the earth,
how even the watching hawk drops to the mouse,
how unresistingly the fat figs fall;
come down into the sun and feed and die.

But you sit with your back turned to the sky
and look at your own shadow and the shadow
cast by the mortared stones along the earth
a little way. Behind you in the light
wide slopes drop down under the terrace wall
down where the warm grapes spill their seed and die.

What holds you thus encumbered, stubborn? Why
do you sit dark against the morning's shimmer,
cold to the green seductions of the earth
lulling you down towards her possible lap?
When did the winter blind about you fall
that shuts you from the sun where breed and die

foxes, mice, hawks, the myriad progeny
of every fruit that swells only to wither?
I was dismembered from the plangent earth,

turned from the country of her innocence,
longer ago than any hills recall.
I know the hawk's drop, know the greed to die

of living as the foxes die, but I
am trapped above the light by an old knowledge
too late to shed. I carry in the earth
a burden heaviest among the fields
of summer where the poppies fade and all
the ears of doomed wheat slake their need to die

but not my need. Call it a memory,
a grievous memory that I was born to,
not to be hidden in the hiding earth,
of how I lost her, how I was sent out,
pitched from her mortal garden once for all
to reaches whence no man is freed to die.

Nevertheless, though caught against the sky,
caught fast from time inside the little darkness
that clouds my head and keeps me from the earth,
I know at its deep quick a different love,
a love more punctual, kind and prodigal
than death's own love, and do not plead to die.

I

Subiaco

Drop to the floor the wild flowers you have cut
and empty-handed let the lily soar,
the flame in you the dark will not put out,
the angel said, give him your pain, your fear,
your flesh, that in you his earth may receive
the everlasting word that made it home,
and to the same call in a mountain cave
a monk answer · secundum verbum tuum
fiat mihi. We are cradled in his death
the white sky without angels drying his blood
filled · flowing in the mystery of God
that holds · feeds all who turn to him in faith
like hers who to anoint him for his grave
undid her jar, her hair, undid her love.

II

Horace's farm

Clover and cyclamen and linnet song
and nut tree shadows littering the spring,
his bowl of grass, water, thyme, poplars, set
down in the Sabine hills, their soft lines cut
to the clean edge of his resourcefulness
nimium brevis · aere perennius
mild words he touched · and held · minding their bloom
handfuls of flowers remembered in hot Rome
among rich treacherous men empty of God
as he, his even soul knowing the light
snuffed in the black river, the walnut shell
rocking downstream into death's long exile,
his only glimpse of paradise restored
the great dog Cerberus licking his feet.

Looking and seeing

Ergo vide me, Domine; vides et scis, vide ut sciam. St Anselm

I

Do you believe in the son of man?
Who is he? said the man born blind.
You are looking at him.

Light for the eyes of the heart
breaks in the darkness of God
looking for us · for her

to give him flesh in which
his clouded sons might see
his glory visible

our flesh in which to die
our blood in which to shed
our infidelity

he looked on her to bear
the living body of God
the killed body of God

the body that bears us home
in, through, the death he died
in, through, the life he gave

fiat mihi secundum verbum tuum
your son · God's flesh and blood
sicut in caelo et in terra
          fiat in me.

II

Looking for him at the Pasch
twenty years too soon
the soldier's careless lance
a needle at her heart
she found him in the temple
          post triduum
questioning the wise.
          Mulier quid ploras?
Did you not know I have things
of my father's to do?

(There is a cage which you will make yourself
with help no doubt · but you will slide the bolt
alone and find it stuck fast and the bars
rusted tight down and heavy on your soul
self-forged · unshakeable · the gates of Sheol
and from that night seven devils will laugh at you.)

When he read from the book of God
'I have come to give sight to the blind
to those in prison freedom
to the broken-hearted joy'
they saw · they were looking at him.

How except through his death
could the God of Abraham
enter the night of Sheol
undo the infinite cages?

With Mary his mother and John
you are looking for him at the Pasch
at the hanged body of God
given for the life of the world
beloved Christ · who tore
seven devils out of you.

From the ruins of the temple
God has gone
has left

the daughter of the city
cries · Where is corn and wine?
looking for him.

He is in Sheol
silenced the word of God
among the silent dead.

III

Mulier quid ploras?
In Sheol I have been among the lost
lost of my father · and alone of him.

Why do you look for me among the dead?
    Did I not tell you
the spoilers of his garden killed his son
        once and for all?

He will not leave his holy one in Sheol.
    I said to the thief · Today
you will be with me in paradise
the bars of your cage blown feathers
        lost on the wind of God.

IV

And she told them · I have seen him.

Can the meaning of everything be declared
in a morning garden to a woman in tears
looking for him · not seeing him?

On a country road where a stranger talks
to a pair of travellers · looking for him
not seeing him?

In the breaking of bread?

Why are you crying?

One by one
slow hearts to burn
I am looking for you
from the foundation of the world.

V

Through glaciers, fossils and millennia,
the quiet collisions of the furthest stars,
the civilisations and the centuries,
through years and days, the hours, the seconds,
        looking for you
        is nothing else.

The word promised among the prophets' words,
gleams among answers to the great questions,
justice and mercy in the names of gods,
your darkness and your light consuming theirs –

no metaphor, no analogue, no sign
of you, for you, but you your very self
        O Christ of God

your goodness, truth and beauty measuring
the quality of every good and truth
we think we see, of every love that pulls
the eddying soul into your powerful flood.

God can do anything
        and what he does
from the foundation of the world is give
        himself.

Sonnet for Christmas

'A film on the life of Archbishop Romero has been bought for private distribution by the Roman Catholic church. It was turned down by all the major American television networks on the grounds that it is too depressing and devoid of a love interest.' News item on Advent Sunday

This is my body, my sense of the earth
you made me, feet on the stony ground, eyes
the flames of new wheat catch, flesh from my birth
learning the touch of things, how the land lies
to the sun and the knife strengthens the vine,
learning from millstone, winepress, wince of smashed
flesh, offering to death raised hands, yours, mine,
over the kneeling people fresh blood splashed,
nails driven between sinews, hammered through
as bullets to the heart the wrists' hollows,
so that the breaking of the bread, the stain
of the spilt cup seeping through dust hallows
your dry world and its desert souls like rain.
This is my body given up for you.

Leonardo at Amboise: Easter 1519

As a boy he would watch the river suck
and dump continually twisting its thread
now with but now against the grain, the rock
of things swung in the water's cut and thrust
for ever as far as he could see from first
springing the mountainside like milk like seed
out to the roar and crash of the stormtide
making and breaking into mud, sand, dust
for wind in turn to take and to forsake
and flood to scatter to infinity.

A quality weight had, force a desire,
that seeing eye and agile hand could scale,
quarry, unbind, tap, draft to the mind's rule,
all flow become cause and effect of power.
In the high Apennines he came on shells;
by what compulsion was the old sea's floor
hoisted and buckled to these mountaintops
but the same violence that in brooks compels
pebbles to shift and funnelled earth to lapse
into the death that is in liberty?

So much the water taught him and he drew
left handed in his backwards coppery line
water as life, gathered, contained and spilt
in root, vein, twig, gut, dyke, tendril of vine,
fibre of lung, slicing through skin, fat, bone
of putrefying flesh until he knew
sap's streaming channels even as he saw
the marshes' clog and the catch of the silt
that slows the torrent to salt pools and felt
the cataract's death by seepage to the sea.

He watched the river and the just-come swallows
planing; he watched his paralysed left hand
dumb to the bear's pelt that it rested on,
spent as the cracked branch of a stricken tree,
its power run out into the brackish shallows;
the blood in it would crumble in the ground
even as his combed enchanter's beard would soon
bend like the dune-grass to the incoming sea;
he knows the whirlpool's throat open for him,
hears the hills darken to the tempest's drum.

He shuts his eyes against the quick wing beat
of birds his Merlin hand could steady once,
shuts out the gleaming Loire, for the footfall
of something spoken in another sense,
so other that the long-defended will
has held its feared pursuit these fifty years
outside the heart, something not to be caught
in the mind's nets but to be caught by, heard
stalking unlooked-for in baptismal tears
a gift given way to, the passion of God.

Kindless creator and destroyer, moving
beyond the sphere of fire, who gave his son
to a girl's womb, joins all flesh in his own,
alone suffered exacted death that tore
the veil of things, God from himself, and whole
mends riven man for whom light on the eye
homed and the intelligence it kindles are
but shadows of the truth in which we die
blazing, as who on Easter day receives
Christ broken through the locked doors of the soul.

Feast of the Presentation of Our Lady

Pray for us, child of the living God
who will bear him for all of us, his heel
kicking your ribs, his bones hardening, his blood
circling safe in your womb, for us to spill,
the end and the beginning born to die,
to be offered and taken, to be laid
heavy across your lap, three days to lie
in the dark tomb. Obedient child of God
whose altar, like Isaac, they lead you to,
the altar where soon you will bring your child
the sacrifice that God has given for you,
for us, for ever, the light of the world,
the holiness of all who live in God,
                    pray for us.

Jacob

Because all night he fought you
    hurt you to the bone
broke bit by bit like chocolate
    your will into his own
and in the morning left you
    limping · blessed · alone
this once · however briefly
    knowing as you are known
his wound · his name · have marked you
    incurably his own.

The seed that comes to harvest
    on broken ground is sown.

Ithaca Channel
for L.A.R.

An old man sailing home, the light behind him,
recalls that oldest traveller, his ghost;
tired of the desert sun above the sea
and of his knowledge and the not knowing
whether or not he will be known at last,

he studies his advancing shadow, cast
forth on the alien, the familiar sea;
he has returned so late from safer fields,
the Latin limit in the rainy west
where legions came into the upland roads,

monks to the valleys, fetching from this sea
a desert God, and knowledge. Which does he
bring back? Or are they one? Cold Aristotle
blazed in cathedral schools a light that must
be God's: he bent to catch it, call it blest.

He lets that light be darkened in the sea
which had only a human clarity;
in deepening night his shadow will be lost
like his who sailed this way before the past
hoping, doubting, also, that he would find

a certain harbour from the empty sea.
Not that the long-feared, longed-for landfall will
not one day come. It will; and there faith kept
waits for him now, already, or not ever,
secret and patient in the heart of God.

Cede Deo

Infelix, quae tanta animum dementia cepit?
Non viris alias conversaque numina sentis?
Cede Deo.   Aeneid V 465-7

The space between us is the field of God
fine as his secret sword is subtle · wide
as his infinite freedom. In my pocket
a few beads tell the story of all the stories
of woundedness · of need · of man and woman
of fire between us · and the fire between
us and his garden · of action and patience
the only glory is the glory of God
            cede Deo.

Alone she bore the glory of the Lord
the terror of the fatherhood of God
carried his son · his heart · the heart of God
beating in her alongside hers · his flesh
delivered of her flesh · her opened womb
his father's child given for his father's work
his body given for the life of the world
that in our stricken flesh · our griefs and days
            his will be done.

The grief of Dido lost into the fire
the grief of Beatrice and Penelope
waiting for the mysterious other · gone
to fight with God against an enemy sea
to fight even with God · and not let go
to limp back in the dawn · his eyes shadowed
in Troy burning · in the black swamps of hell
where the sad spirits flittered to his hands
        waiting for him.

The one alone · where is he · as she waits
through the long night · fear in her throat for him
wrestling in God · until the angel comes
his friends asleep · looking at one of them
across the wreckage of his constancy
lashed at the pillar · thorns crammed on his head
a beam crushing his shoulder · heavy nails
driven through the sinews of his wrists and feet
        cede Deo.

In his glory · Dante and Beatrice
the river of death between them · walls of fire
between them · but the faithfulness of God
taking their sacrifice into his own
seek out · each other's eyes in paradise
bright from the tears each for the other shed
for the one living · the one dead · who left
care for him printed in the dust of hell
        for him to find.

I have not said to the children of Jacob
to my obedient suffering Aeneas
sailing in guilt from Dido's scornful pyre
or to Penelope · unstitching days
as if time were not telling on her face
her breasts · her hair · seek me in vain · seek me
in chaos · though for their steadfastness · a log
burning hidden in ashes · ancient dark
        muffled my word ·

The only glory is the glory of God
returning in the morning of the world
he brought her back her self · lost into him
her life · she does not know him · and then knows
the mending of her soul in him · his light
never again to be emptied in death
to shine in us · the end he made us for
his given love in undivided hearts
                    made one in him.

Cede Deo.

Schopenhauer sketch

'Without the perceiving subject there is no object'

Rank at the cornfield's edge, fierce, six feet tall,
the great weeds flourish in burning July:
willow-herb, nettles, bracken, thistles like lions,
rusty sorrel, everywhere meadowsweet soft
    to the palm of the hand

and the cream down of the thistle plumes softer still;
all clattery seedheads, spikes, fronds, barbs, prickles, stalks
and the hooks on the barley beards and the

                    new red leaves
of the oaktrees damp from birth – what were
                        they made for
    but the palm of the hand?

Lapis exilis: in Advent

Parzival said: 'Alas, what is God?
Were he mighty, to such derision
he would never have given us over,
could God but live with power.'

The Grail is a stone, its name is lapis exilis. Much has
been written about the meaning and origin of this name
which, as the variant forms of the manuscripts indicate,
bewildered the mediaeval scribes no less than modern
commentators. From Wolfram von Eschenbach's
Parzival, and notes.

I

Lapis exilis
once upon a time
a little stone
under dust
nothing at all

revealed

more precious than gold
grail of the ashes
phoenix stone
dust
of which we shall return

a lexicographical puzzle
among others

lapis ex caelis
lapis exsilii

words can move
us
into and out of exile
of heaven
given up
a crumb of bread
by words become
flesh of our flesh and pain
inhabiting in time our homelessness
the ambiguous tenses
of our constant repetition
he said
this is
which will be
offered and suffered
in time and always

II

The dictionary is heavy with the chippings of authority
displaced a little thing
becomes a great
exacti in exsilium innocentes
savage sentence
look backward as the cart rumbles
but images will not suffice
and who is innocent

old Jews remembering the smell
of furs and frost and tallow
watch in the desert girls with rifles
marching to defend
villages with names their fathers chanted
on Lithuanian sabbaths
or wait for the Pacific night to fall

Ovid beside the reedbeds of the Danube
Solzhenitsyn in Vermont
at liberty to talk barbarian
forbidden therefore to speak
home
is where the censor shreds the typescript

Students in the campus afternoons
admire a ravaged face
not understanding
whose language like a ruined church
speaks fragmentarily
whether by soldiers or neglect
brought to these shards

The unknown cousins live and die
in other dreams than ours
the portraits peasants chopped for kindling
the map of Prussia and the battlefields
graves without flowers

III

ex caelis exsilii exilis lapis
little stone
a mystery
in which the phoenix dies and lives

exile et exiguum et vietum cor
the heart a nut
such as a squirrel might bury against the winter
and forget

the heart a word
for what may be broken
lost
but for where our treasure is
grail of the dust
ex caelis exsilii
little stone

what riches hidden here
go without saying
in the quiet ground
what lyric trees
in these short days
these mists and flaming skies
Christ comes

IV

O holy Spirit like water
cover us
so that when the sun strikes home
we may shine also
stones
in the river's flow

Cleopatra dreams

The dead weight of him was for me to bear
always, across my knees this fallen tree,
the storm that in my lap shed him blown clear
of me, his silence stone enclosing me.
Outside, Caesar's men shout; axes tear wood.
Why should I fear strange knives? His death is mine;
what else? Metal and leather I have peeled
before now from his wounds, starting fresh blood.
Torches smoke; my fingers stick in spilt wine,
who with the Nile his starving desert healed.

'Pone me ut signaculum super
cor tuum'; I took his stamp as wax receives
the seal, matter to form, in deep and mere
response, no more; no more than the poor shell
to the soft powerful flesh which dies and leaves
her empty to the tides, or than the cave
in the roaring night to the fugitive,
the bay that from his last battle could save
the luckier of his scattered ships, the bell
he struck; I am cast of him and shall not live.

The withering of the snapped bough: I shall die
in the parched winter of my absolute need
carrying him in grief, his mastery
taxing mouthful by mouthful my life's breath
for the fruit I fed him once. Who shall lead
us from our ashy underworld where each
to the other's blinded touch is lost in death?
His hand stiffens and his crushing body,
no longer his nor mine, chills; on what beach
of dwindling dust does he stand calling me?

The snake at my breast sips my strength to sleep,
pillows the flaring night. Slipped from my lap
the load of him eases, is eased. They wash
with oil his wounds, and from his broken flesh
loosen the scabs; with myrrh they come to wrap
him for his burial where the soldiers keep
their watch in vain. Who is it that believes
what I shall see? In man and woman spring,
freedom from power: between us a sapling
uncurls to the first day its bright sweet leaves.

Vespers

Not many words you might suppose
for use thus regular and intent.
You might expect the centuries
of hours and days to have worn
them smooth and small like pebbles
beneath the always moving sea,
the living and dying of men whose prayer
has broken above them on the shifting beach:

a spring of water · rams and sacrifice
mountains · dew · the leaping hills
shepherd and tents
millstones and the young ravens
dust · honey · salt
and the scattering of enemies –

they have become a forest of huge trees
through which collected voices move
regular and intent in change and change
of notes as few as bells
hunting God
and in their deep shade find the glare of truth
slivers of sunlight on the quiet ground.

THE MYSTERIES
OF THE ROSARY

I

The Annunciation

Once only · across lilies · to the core
of mystery · of making · of the power
of God in Trinity · after · before
the silent consonance of that single hour
a girl was called to answer in consent
the terror of his glory covering her
his fathering spirit asking to be lent
our mortal flesh and blood · our earth · in her
breaking open the kingdom of his son
so that the word through whom all things were made
should be conceived in her · his will be done
in any of us · however afraid
of suffering ahead · the dark we pray
his angel will light for us as his way.

II

The Visitation

Left by the angel in her silent day
alone to bear the spoken word of God,
for company · for human touch · she fled,
the light of the dark world shadowed away
in her, waiting in her for winter birth,
crushed as the flames of leaves are crumpled up
in sticky chestnut buds, as in one pip
petals and apples sleep under the earth.

She fled for comfort · and discovered praise
in her own mouth · his glory recognised
in her · who had already given to God
in her obedient suffering of his grace
his mortal flesh · his touch · his death · his blood
let free to free us to her life in Christ.

III

The Nativity

The angels sing elsewhere; beyond her sight
the star shines for the travellers of the earth;
she hears only his breathing in the night
of peace, safely himself, the shock of birth
safely cried through, the cord cut, his heart's blood
no longer beating in her, sealed, his own.
She brushes corn out of the harmless wood,
wraps him in cloth and lays him down alone.
No one has brought myrrh yet. The puzzled beasts
watch over him, a perfect baby, lulled,
as she is, in their munching warmth. Her breasts
are heavy with the coming milk; she rests
near him in the soft dark, God's sleeping child
whose child is born for the life of the world.

IV

The presentation of Christ in the temple

A sign that will undo the enemy
in each of us · a candle in our cave
for us (choosing instead the secrecy
of our sufficient dark) to stifle · love
asking of each of us all that we have
entrusted to our dangerous liberty
to close on as our own · or else to give
with grace from time to his eternity:

have eyes to see this six-weeks child · a sword
his judgement splintering the artifice
we hide in from the power of his word
Israel receives the glory of the Lord
whose body will be given in sacrifice
to bring us out of death to paradise.

V

The finding of Christ in the temple

Flesh of her flesh · though every mother's son
has from his birth her loss in him · this loss
before the life he came for has begun
terrifies her · the shadow of his cross
hardens · unknowing she practises her grief
till the third day. Among strange crowds they seek
him down long pilgrim roads without relief.

God said I lift my child against my cheek.

In the circle of listeners her fears
discover the conviction in his eyes.
'My father's house.' Only his mother hears
his words fall · pebbles · in her well of tears.

The doctors of the law · not enemies
yet · do not ask 'Who does he think he is?'

VI

Gethsemane

Rescue my soul from the sword – Psalm 21

The sword that draws his sweat like amber blood
finds between God and man the Spirit's space
opens in him the wound in Adam seared
our mortal scar · the channel for his grace.
In the darkened garden · companionless
bound to the freedom of a twisting blade
he knows that he can · and cannot · let pass
this cup · his · their · our flesh · paled from the word
he is · until his father's will is his.

Before he wakes them · as the soldiers come
ordinary-weaponed · that his will be done
the angel at the gate of paradise
who bars the tree of life · lays down his sword
crossing the garden for the son of God.

VII

The scourging of Christ

If you were looking for him you could look
all day and never find him · not a sign
no followers · no arguers · no sick
begging for health · sight · hearing · he has gone
into the veil of broken flesh · the dark
of blindfolded flogging. Who hit you then?
And then? The lash whistles. And then? They mock,
used soldiers bored to the routine of pain
that scatters mobs. Weals blossom on his neck
matching their plaited cords. Crowds cheered him in,
surrendered hero on a donkey's back,
and have forsaken him. I shall strike down
the shepherd of my flock · and I shall rise
and go before you into Paradise.

VIII

The crowning with thorns

In ribaldry their powerless king is crowned,
stripped for imperial purple tatters, shoved
to sway unsteady on a stool, and found
a reed for rule over the world God loved.
The bent and twisted thorntwigs they cram down
into his scalp; blood trickles down his eyes
like tears, whitefaced, mute, guyed, a circus clown
ringed with the catcalls of his enemies:

the unheard music of the spheres is his.
Out of the clamour we have hidden him in
his silence speaks across our cruelties
who gathers to himself all human grief,
suffers and offers every human sin
and, bleeding, bears it towards the gates of life.

IX

Christ carries his cross

Where I am going you cannot follow me
nor · if I told you · would you yet believe
the weight I bear is your neglect of me
your glance elsewhere · your head turned from my love
for you · whenever · you may look at me
stumbling these stony streets · sweat mixed with blood
the hardness of your hearts laid heavy on me
my gibbet · great nailed beams of splintered wood.

Two thousand years I climb this cruel hill
day after day you have remembered me
and turned away from where · still · at the still
quick of you · dying · I call you home to me
who went before you so that · if you will
where I am going you might follow me.

X

Crucifixion

Crossed at the quick of death's long history
two splintered planks nailed up for him to bear
labelled in irony · the place to die
for all of us · his love let pour out where
time's dusty kernel splits to eternity
et nunc et semper · pulse of every prayer
that beats at the heart of his Trinity
hidden in this his pasch · from us · from her

child of her suffering him her virgin blood
begotten and forsaken of the God
whose murdered body hangs on the raw wood
that cuts our shoulders · whose word to be shed
even as he takes in his pierced hands our bread
harrows with light the silence of the dead.

XI

Resurrection

Videbunt in quem transfixerunt

Towards first light she who had watched him die
came through her empty world in tears · her love
wrapped with his broken body in the grave ·
to tend his cold corpse · she had heard his cry
forsaken on the cross they had made him carry
and mourned him · hanging dead as the dead wood
they nailed him to · she had seen water and blood
flow from him · who now quietly called her · Mary.

On the same day · the first · the stone rolled back
(is not my word the hammer that splits rock?)
two walked with him · not seeing him · and heard
not understanding him · (is not my word
him they have pierced?) · until he broke their bread
broke his life free to all with eyes to look.

XII

Ascension

Why are you gazing at the empty sky?
Quietly · as quietly as he took · one bright
March day · his mother's flesh · our flesh · he takes
back to his father · beyond touch and sight
our sight · our touch · our healed humanity.
The cloud of his mysterious going cracks
still · to his everlastingness · his light
the shining silence of the Trinity
he broke · to bear through his death ours also
his sheaves · the harvest of his world he came
to reap in glory · carrying us home.

My word shall not return to me empty;
where he is · all I have given him shall be.
Paravi lucernam Christo meo.

XIII

Pentecost

Prayer is an empty womb. We wait with her
through whose obedience to his spirit · his will
he took our flesh. Husks for the burning · still
(bridal her stillness) we must learn from her
her suffering of him · Christ to become
in us his word spoken · our tongues of fire
racing through dusty straw of old desire
smarting in Plato's eyes · the one to come
into our darkened senses · to be killed
for his truth's light · not to be left in death
but raised among us to the glory of God
that the world's blazing fields may yet be filled
with new corn. Seed and spirit and fire and breath
of life · speak also in our flesh and blood.

XIV

Assumption

She to whom God gave grace for her to live
in consonance with him · her will to his
tuned as a single note · that she might give
him body and blood to give in death for us
dies into his new life. Born free of sin
to walk in Eden light · in clarity
that at our hearts' far reach we can begin
to listen for through the deafening fury
of our will against his · until there breaks
into the oneness of his sacrifice
our brittle pride · she dies. For her alone
he opens wide the gates of paradise
so long shut · and the second Adam takes
back to his side the flesh that is his own.

XV

The Coronation of Our Lady

Where is she now · our mother and his bride?
Her child given up to death · his body · his blood
in his priest's hands for us · the love he died
to pour into our lives · her son · our God
who trod the desert in the flesh she fed
the space from God of his mortality
whose faithfulness is told among the dead
as Easter time cracks to eternity –

where is she now? Other than him · his own
as we may be · among the saints she led
out of their sins in the power of her prayers
the light of his Jerusalem her crown
the city of all he fetches from the dead
to light beyond the sun and the other stars.

Backwater time

I

Birdsong · rocks · oaktrees · quick water
a clearing
into which Bernard and his thirty knights
jingle one morning · out of which
after some hours yeomen will ride bemused
each leading
a saddled horse laden with bright clothes · thinking
the young masters mad

acorns on the forest floor

ancestral habit of silence and the dark

under the oaktrees · troutbecks
rattling from high hills
flies over dangerous pools in summer
black ice water in February
colder than the snow

monks brought God here in their words and hands
into the wolves and mistletoe and snow
bread · wine · some books · two bits of wood · word of
a winter baby and a death in spring

later they built a church

later it fell

they are not gone

the spirits of the living and the dead
in the spaces between prayer
mutter together of God
one by one
they reach the desert
of wild honey

trees and stones will teach you · Bernard said
what masters cannot

II

a bent for the transcendent
the margin where the one flame
consumes the dark about it
as Liszt's last music note by note the silence
Beethoven hearing what he cannot hear
Milton scenting paradise unlost
in the landscape of the blind

always now on the real edge
the edge of the real where the more real
starts like pigeons flying in golden light
where a piece of bread becomes the body
of God in a man's hands
to live
in days that rhyme
and years

believing the recovery of innocence
after all at the heart possible
after all
a gift
one to the other but of God
Cordelia to Lear

III

Quomodo cantabimus canticum Domini in terra aliena?

As from a high hill scoured by ice and the moor wind
where flesh lapses from a dead ram's horned skull
as earth from rock · and slow burn bracken encroaches
where among thistles and fallen walls
seeddrill and plough rust under wormy rafters
ivy flourishes over the cowbyre stones
nettles where dead men lugged pails · yelled at dogs
and women sewed by candles and the bowling stars
and warmed lambs wrapped in old coats by their fire
        to know the world redeemable
        redeemed

When the shadows of the half known · half perceived
gain on the day · the year · and the solstice-shallow sun
drops at three under the high sky line · the paled west
leeching light from the moor · from the secret farms
and the winter river roars through the broken weir
while the cows stand still as the stone walls
that measure the grazing fields of shepherds buried
a century under tilted gravestones
        down the dale

sing in your blood and bone · your self forgotten
in the no more strange because
his also promised land
        the song of God.

IV

backwater time
where willow leaves float
so slowly they might
have fallen in Eden
did anything fall there

from the dorter window
look down a long way
to the choir · a well
empty of voices
two iron bars
keep you from falling

a boy is drawing
an empty church
exacting in fine
ink lines like these
no shadows of the shadowy
huge arches

he is a photograph
nobody took
drawing from the life
of stones like trees
he makes · being young
no mistakes

the dusk grows thick
crowding the arches
to a dark wood
outside the swifts
scream over fishponds
eight hundred summers

the monks are gone
no more than the boy
leaves
backwater time
lives
in the hand of God.

Sestina on All Souls Night: Rievaulx

'This is the original evil, that man regards himself as his own light' St Augustine

Perhaps there is a history of silence,
even an anecdote, from which we learn
distinctions that have much to to with dying
and something of the point at which our broken
minutes, the funnelled sand we are, may cross
eternity as the dust moon the light

of the earth-hidden sun. Out of this light,
three times reflected, reaching our eyes broken
to mist three times from the first day and dying
each time in radiance, tonight could we learn
to suffer the search of the word whose silence
bleeds on the heavy gibbet of the cross?

Shall we not build a castle of the cross,
chivalric in the desert of our broken
skill at living, stone by squared stone – and learn
that what we learn must crumble to the light
over again of God's destroying silence?
What can we know that will not lapse, a dying

of each assurance of the self, the dying
of all our subtle registers which cross
the moonlit space between us with their broken
declarations, their images of light,
mirrors that flaw and shatter into silence?
It is to unlearn always that we learn.

Though what we know we need is still to learn
(catching on western slopes of talk a light
we take for ours), the sense we make is dying.
Listen to the great ruined church, the cross
of singing arches smashed to rocks of silence
blacker than the soft woods, hauled down and broken.

On this night of the flocking dead, the broken
and healed, can we from men who shaped their dying
in steadied days among these stones not learn
courage to live where time and grace do cross,
because, in the wreck terror charred, the light
is gentle also as the fall of silence?

O God whose flesh was broken on the cross
so that we should not learn by our own light
reach us, the dying, with your sword of silence.

Paolo Uccello's Hunt in a Forest

They ride for the heart
of the world's wood
slender the treetrunks
and darkness after
bright day behind
hounds in cry
trample the lilies
break for the quarry
the riders after.

What are they after?
the wild boar
that will turn and tear them?
The white doe that will die
and leave them silent
bloody-handed as they look
one to another?
The unicorn that is never found
unless he lie
in the lap of a girl?
The Holy Grail?
They will not know
till the hunt is over.

Ride for the heart
of the world's wood.

The time before you die

Look inwards from the time before you die:
Find out of time a place to be, a cave
Where from the darkness you can bear the sky.

Even as you watch the day-long butterfly
Quiver among the scents the summer gave,
Look inwards from the time before you die.

Cathedral glass distracts to harmony
The simple light. Kneel down in the cold nave,
So that from darkness you may bear the sky.

Or love will stay you: under the reply
Of other eyes you see the hope you crave
Look inwards from the time before you die.

Believe, believe there is no unheard cry
Though every throat will founder in the grave
For into darkness you must bear the sky.

The candle gutters that you travel by,
The shadows crowd upon the hour you have,
Yet here is all the time before you die
And from time's darkness you shall bear the sky.

Peterborough – Ely 10.40

Caught from the train in certain morning light
the black-monk abbeys of the fens survive
junk cars, paint warehouses, the parking lot
behind Asda. On their canals swans move
coupled to their reflections and the sky
is quiet in water only, split with planes
sent shattering from Suffolk. Where's the sea
flooding the levels, where are the high skeins
of Baltic geese? With Hereward the Wake,
Catherine of Aragon, all the dead monks.
From the train windows a few strangers look
at ploughed earth, pylons, tractors; the eye blinks
tears at the sudden silences of stone
collected in, for, God, their office gone.

Ladyswell

(where St Ninian baptised in the 5th century)

Crowded with silence as the air
    angels always choose
a pool in the grey Northumbrian hills
    blood on a bird's breast

out of the rocks baptismal water
    bubbling · still · as time
passing and held in the hand of God
    his Easter fire lit

however neat the gate · the roses
    love wastefully poured
cracks open the grave's separateness
    to the lucky dead.

Monks renew their vows

There's no accounting otherwise for this
extravagance, this hurling of the best
wine over desert sand, what a man is,
the heart of him, demanded, sacrificed
again, in steadfastness, in fire burning
lifelong the insistent self, the enemy
resentful as Satan of God' s turning
our fallen flesh towards eternity
in Christ his Son; heaven and hell have split
without a sound in you, for he who spins
in ice the furthest planet and its moons
and hears them crack has seen you as you sat
under a figtree and not let you be;
his work your difficult fidelity.

His other time

The other time we live in
is not our own · nor even
time · ticking condition
of tiring flesh · but gift
his own present · presence
in us · at his own choosing.

Someone in whose memory
the past like a promise
is kept · kneels at a window
listening to the dark
tick its quiet occasions
next to the skin:

the pulse of the beck
water against stones
bickering a little
ducks on the pond
owls from old woods
calling · a fox;

sounds of the night
next to the skin.
In the same valley
(undo his kindness
from the stacked pile)
Aelred lies buried

near the wrecked altar
eight hundred years
safe from the sea.
He heard the owls and foxes
in the ticking night
while his monks slept;

in his hands a book
carried for solace
across time's sea
the life of one dead
in Roman Africa
eight hundred years.

What did he have
Augustine for Aelred?
Clean fierce linen
next to the skin
the story of a love
that was never enough

in time · but was
and is God's sabbath.
She shuts the window
goes · like them
to sleep alone · her bed
a barque for the sea

Rehearsing death
prayer in their company
holds her folded
close as their days
kept in his memory
his other time.

On Hadrian's Wall

D M

CORN.VICTOR S.C.
MIL.ANN. XXVI
CIV.PANNON.
VIX.ANN.LV D.XI
CONIUX PROCURAVI

D M, dis manibus, cut in cold stone;
to unforgiving spirits she let him go,
his dust into a northern winter blown
as flakes of snow are. What else could she do?
Down long imperial roads there had not come
word that the harrowing radiance of the truth
had lit to nothingness the gods of Rome.
As one the rivers of his age and youth
raced in his blood, old Danube springs the same
ice cracking as black Tyne's. Fifty five years
eleven days he lived, into whose name
hers, crystals on his coat, melts, disappears.
Suscipe eos, God of the living, who said
we should not look for you among the dead.